Gorillas!
An Animal Encyclopedia for Kids (Monkey Kingdom)
Children's Biological Science of Apes & Monkeys Books

PRODIGYWIZARD
BOOKS

Do you want to discover amazing facts about gorillas? Have you seen one in your entire life?

Kids, meet the world's largest primates- the gorillas.

Do you know that gorillas build nests on which they sleep? Yes, they spend most of their time on the ground, although they also build nests in the trees. They build nests on the ground every night.

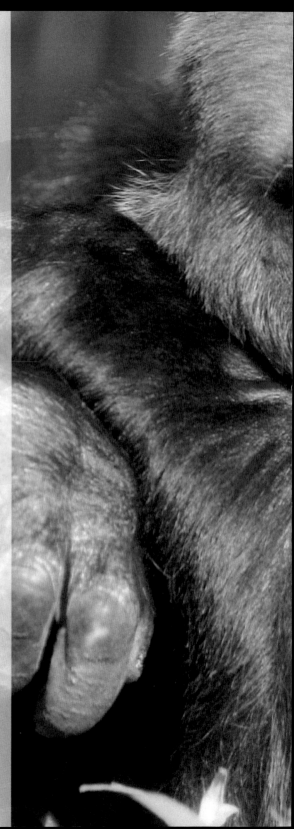

A dominant male, called silverback, leads the troop. He can be identified by the gray strip of hair on his back.

Gorillas live in groups called troops or bands. Each band could have a maximum of 50 members and a minimum of two members.

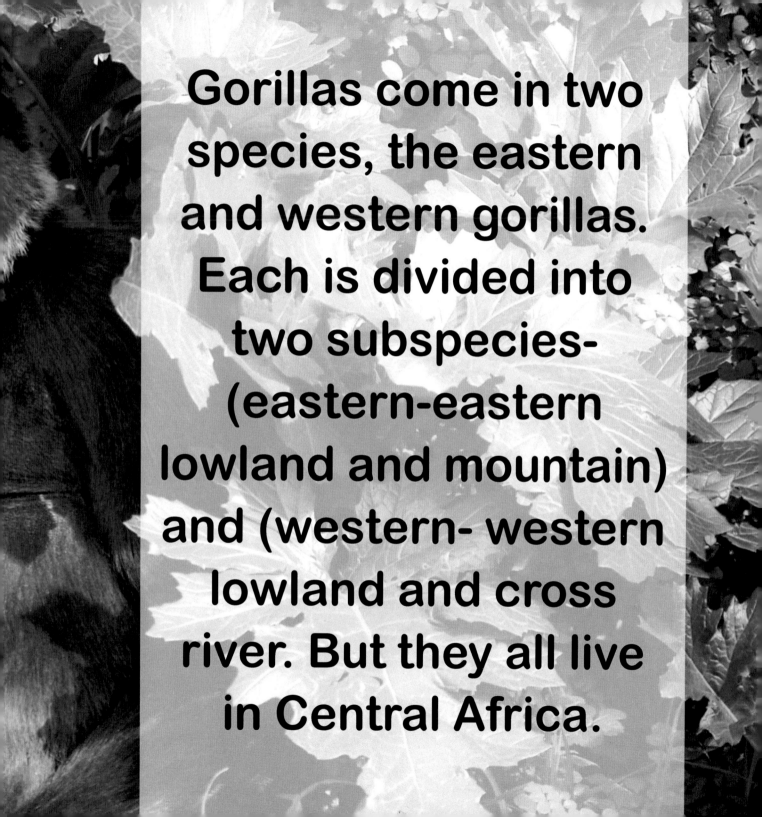

Gorillas come in two species, the eastern and western gorillas. Each is divided into two subspecies- (eastern-eastern lowland and mountain) and (western- western lowland and cross river. But they all live in Central Africa.

The most numerous of the subspecies is the western gorilla and the least numerous is the cross river gorilla.

Gorillas are closely related to humans. They are considered intelligent like humans. They are capable of using tools and they can use different means of communication. They can produce 25 different sounds.

Do you know Koko?

Koko was a famous captive-born gorilla. When she was a year old, she was taught sign language. When she was 40 years old, she could understand some 2,000 English words.

Gorillas are herbivores, which means that they only eat plants. They roam around and spend their day looking for fruits and leafy plants. Do you know that an adult gorilla can eat up to 30kg of food every day?

Gorillas have a slow reproduction rate. Every four to six years, a female gorilla can produce only one baby and gives birth three or four times in her existence. She starts giving birth at about 10 years old.

Like humans, gorillas wait nine months before a baby can be born. They give birth to one baby gorilla at a time. Their babies usually weigh approximately 4 pounds. Their development is, however, twice as fast as that of humans.

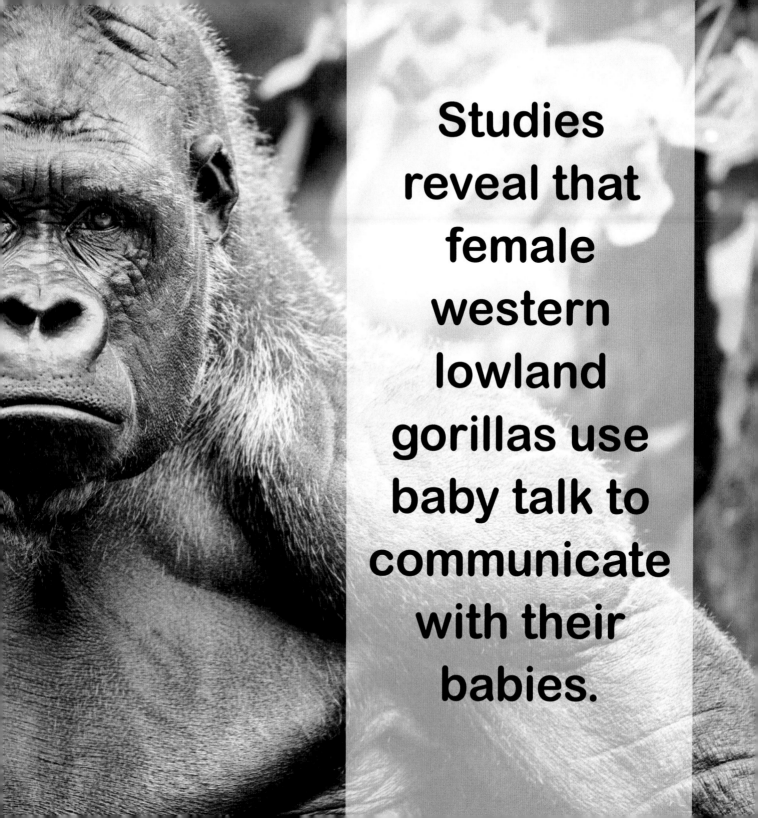

Studies reveal that female western lowland gorillas use baby talk to communicate with their babies.

Gorillas walk using their knuckles and legs. Their arms are longer than their legs. They can weigh 500 pounds and can be 6ft tall.

Gorillas have 5 toes on each foot and five fingers on each hand. They use gestures, sounds, body postures, and slapping their chests to communicate. Studies reveal that gorillas are not aggressive. They are shy animals.

Like humans,
gorillas
also display
individual
personalities.
They are
capable of
showing what
they feel.

Gorillas can groom themselves. They groom each other using their fingers and teeth.

There is more to know about the gorillas. Research and have fun!